BARS, CLUBS & LOUNGES

SIBYLLE KRAMER

BARS, CLUBS & LOUNGES

BRAUN

CONTENTS

PREFACE

The first clubs were opened in the USA in the 1930s, with a jukebox for an evening of dancing. The term "discotheque" goes back to the Greek word "discos", or disc and "théke" for container. The resemblance in French to the word "bibliothèque" (library) is not to be overlooked, because that is actually how the first harbor clubs were used for a while in Marseille at the beginning of the 1940s: sailors deposited their favourite records with the clubs in order to be able to hear them again when they returned. After the Second World War the clubs took off in France and in England. Today they are a part of every urban landscape, which they change with the onset of night. As the sun goes down, the colored lights of the bars, clubs and lounges stage their own special atmosphere, inviting patrons to enjoy themselves. Every location strives to be unique, with a variety that seems inexhaustible. For example, the Allure by Cipriani from Orbit Design Studio features a mood of glamour with sharply contoured geometric elements on the ceiling and walls, which together with the colorful play of light flooding the space, exude energy and inspiration. In contrast, soft forms and light-colored materials create an oasis of calm, providing the appropriate setting to tune out and relax, as the bar in the Hilton Pattaya, designed by the Department of Architecture and Dazzle Design demonstrates. Soft, swinging ceiling elements extending into the floor as lines surround the space in a poetic atmosphere, conveying strength and quiet.

As different as the bars selected here may be, they all share a pronounced conceptual approach and rigorous realization. The design of the dominant ceiling, responsible for good acoustics and an important base for the lighting, extends to the walls and influences the design of furniture and installations. These holistic approaches are capable of beaming us into another world, as Foster + Partners have done to perfection in the Atrium Champagne Bar: the enormous volume of the space, a pyramid whose pinnacle lets in light sparkling like a diamond, is executed with high-quality materials and a unified color concept. The jellyfish motif projection, extricated from its usual geometrical context, creates a theatrical world, where one gladly immerses oneself.

Every club, bar and lounge has its own recipe for a mood it offers us far away from the routine. The spaces and scenes allow us to immerse ourselves in musical sounds, or create the quiet for clear thinking and relaxed discussion. Or they let the beat pound through the body and propel us onto the dance floor. Visions flowing from architecture and design with fantastical concepts mediate the transfer into these worlds.

The space for the hotel lobby and bar occupies the 16th floor, high above the bustle of Pattaya beach below. The architectural intervention to the entire ceiling plane, with its dynamic wave lines, leads the movement of the visitors towards the seafront beyond. The fabric installation on the ceiling becomes a main feature in the space while simple elements on the ground provide a tranquil atmosphere. At night, strip lighting accents the linear fabric pattern from above. At the end of the lobby space the bar area is arranged with maximum opening to the ocean view. The backdrop is a wooden wall with alcoves where the daybeds are partially tucked into the wall. Further in front of the indoor bar area is an outdoor lounge space with a large pond reflecting both the sky and the droplet daybeds and lamps placed around the pond.

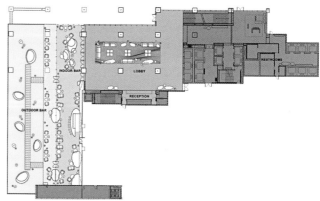

HILTON PATTAYA

You don't need to go to the beach to experience
the movement of the waves – the poetry of this
design enchants and envelopes the space.

Interior architect | Department of ARCHITECTURE
Lighting designer | Dazzle Design
Location | Pattaya, Thailand
Size | 3,100 sqm
Completion | 2010
Type | lounge & bar

INSTALAÇÃO NIGHT CLUB

A journey through color and light – Spatial boundaries disappear, generating an utterly unique atmosphere.

Interior designer | José Carlos Cruz
Location | Porto, Portugal
Size | 250 sqm
Completion | 2013
Type | club

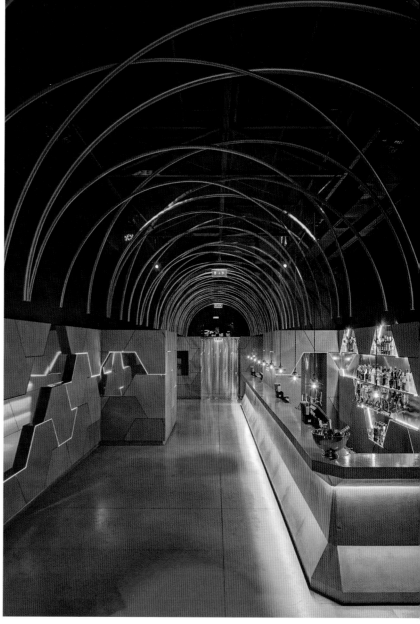

The pre-existing main space was a long and quite narrow room, divided by two structural arches that support the building. The two arches suggest a tunnel linking the whole space. Inspired by an Olafur Eliasson installation, the result was a golden wired tunnel that seems to float. This structure provided the club with the name: "Instalação" (Installation). The space is surrounded by concrete walls whose stereotomy is punctuated by brass surfaces that contrast with the industrial environment. The smaller VIP room was inspired by Andy Warhol's Factory. The acoustic ceiling resembles some Anish Kapoor interventions. This club is located in the nightlife district of Porto.

13

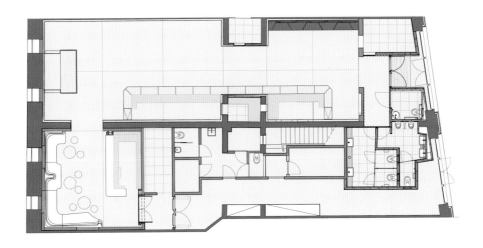

The 5-star ME London is the first hotel in which the design of everything, from the shell of the building to the layout of the public spaces and guest rooms has been undertaken by the Foster studio. The bold geometry of the structure has been exploited to dramatic spatial effect, reinforcing a sense of architectural cohesion between the interiors and exterior. Arriving guests pass through the ground floor lounge and ascend to a dedicated hotel lobby and champagne bar on the first floor located within the soaring volume of a nine-story-high pyramid. Clad in white marble, and naturally lit from above, the pyramid engenders a strikingly theatrical sense of arrival. The pyramid volume at the heart of the triangular plan generates an efficient floor layout, culminating in a generous roof garden and bar terraces.

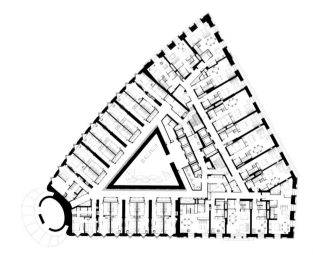

Architect | Foster + Partners
Location | London, UK
Completion | 2012
Type | bar & lounge

A fascinating interplay of ecclesiastical spatial proportions, a modern setting, high-quality materials and foreign elements. No better way to enjoy Champagne.

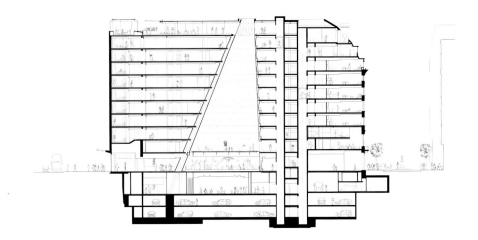

AVENUE CLUB AT CAFE MOSKAU

Architect | studio karhard®
Location | Karl-Marx-Allee 34, Berlin, Germany
Size | 600 sqm
Completion | 2013
Type | club

Cafe Moskau was built at the beginning of the 1960s near Alexanderplatz as the trend-setting crown jewel of an ensemble including a restaurant and entertainment complex. It represents the pinnacle of the most modern DDR architecture. After the fall of communism the former night bar in the cellar was used as a party location. The stipulation for the reconstruction was to install a permanent club in rooms which were not regularly used in the night bar. The access to the club is through the historically protected foyer and staircase into a hallway whose wall features a light object made of 150 wall lights. This hallway leads to a foyer furnished with a wooden wall with slits, with leather and metal furniture in shades of red and orange. The dance floor is framed by decorative wall elements made of woven strips of stainless steel and brass.

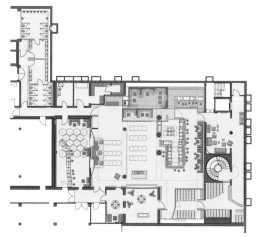

"Who said nights were for sleep?" –
Marilyn Monroe, American actress and singer

STUDIO HERMES

Studio Hermes is a club and restaurant featuring a variety of shows, from cabaret to live bands. Because of the acoustic requirements the design has the look of a 1960s audition hall. Other design elements, while contemporary, follow the same mid-century modern line. The onyx bar, velvet sofas, brass cymbals and walnut wainscot counterpoint the bare concrete and exposed pipes. Studio Hermes is located in Bucharest's historical center and takes its name from an old movie theater that was formerly located at the same address.

Interior designer | Corvin Cristian in collaboration with Vlad Hani
Size | 600 sqm
Location | Selari Street, Bucharest, Romania
Completion | 2013
Type | club & restaurant

"Basically, I'm for anything that gets you through the night – be it prayer, tranquilizers or a bottle of Jack Daniels." – Frank Sinatra, American singer

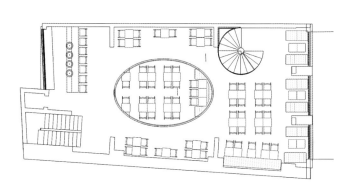

LE MERIDIEN ZHENGZHOU

Stars sparkle in the firmament and transform the space into an oasis of night.

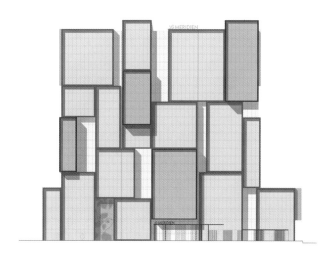

Architect | Neri&Hu
Location | Zhengzhou, Henan province, China
Size | 43,000 sqm total area
Completion | 2013
Type | hotel, lounge, bar & restaurant

Le Meridien Hotel is a new landmark for Zhengzhou, the capital of Henan province, by the Shanghai-based firm, Neri&Hu. The 25-story building consists of a 5-story podium of public functions and a tower of 350 guestrooms. The allusion to excavation and carving which refer to the nearby historic Longmen Caves is expressed in the various openings surrounding the central atrium that visually connect the public spaces across multiple floors. Skylights highlight the sedimentary pattern on the grey sandstone clad walls. The hotel features three restaurants: In the Japanese restaurant the ceiling of walnut boxes shifts in both height and size, with several of the largest dropping low enough to form semi-private dining rooms. The Chinese restaurant private dining rooms are a series of black mesh volumes extending into the all-day dining restaurant through strategic cuts in the floor.

"The use of free time makes the difference between living and existing." – American proverb

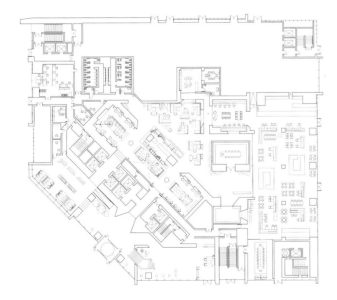

ALLURE BY CIPRIANI

Nautical chic meets up with urban design in a unique world in a maritime setting.

Architect and interior designer | Orbit Design Studio
Location | Yas Island, Abu Dhabi
Size | 1,000 sqm
Completion | 2010
Type | club

Allure is the first nightclub by the legendary Cipriani restaurateurs. Bearing in mind the pedigree of Cipriani and its location on the exclusive Yas Island marina development overlooking the Formula1 race track, this was a project that had to appeal to the highest end of the international luxury crowd. Orbit met and exceeded all expectations with a striking design that combines sensual, nautical inspired seating with fractal walls and ceiling complete with infinite color control in the main room. Pink gold leaf and distinctive bronze cladding add another level of glamour. The terrace overlooks the race track and sports VIP tables for those who really want to indulge. The VIPs enjoy another touch with their own elevator.

33

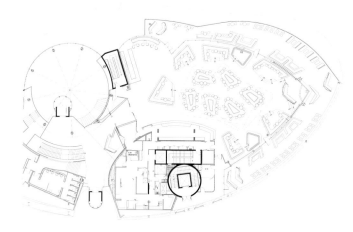

WITWENBALL

Architect | GIORGIO GULLOTTA ARCHITEKTEN
Size | 143 sqm
Location | Weidenallee 20, 20357 Hamburg, Germany
Completion | 2013
Type | bar & restaurant

Witwenball is a stylish, cosy wine restaurant in the popular Schanzenviertel quarter of Hamburg. The project idea is a table for friends and friends of friends. It has a special Paris-Milan flair in the middle of the cool north. The speakeasy feeling which hearkens back to the Roaring Twenties is charged with Italian grandezza. The love for exclusive detail is mirrored in the high-end interior with features like the expansive, imposing counters made of Carrara marble. The tables are fitted with Emperado marble, the benches upholstered with glamorous, turquoise colored material. Fine wallpaper with tender cloud patterns from Italy and an antique mirror wall decorate the walls with a trace of luxury.

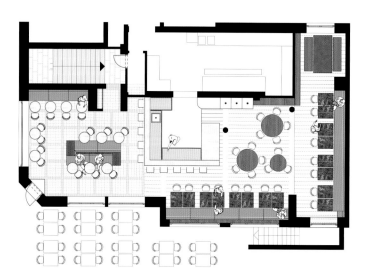

"Art is not the bread of life, it's the wine."
– Jean Paul, German writer

ZEBAR

This is Vertigo 2.0. Sculpturally shaped elements combine the floor, wall and ceiling in an architectonic landscape.

Architect | 3GATTI architecture studio
Location | Shanghai, China
Size | 569 sqm
Completion | 2010
Type | bar

This project was born in 2006 when a Singapore movie director and an ex-musician from south China decided to open a bar in Shanghai. The designer's concept envisioned a caved space formed from a digital Boolean subtraction of hundreds of slices from an amorphous blob. The space was formed in a digital 3D modeling environment, but later subdivided into slices to bring it back from the digital into the real world. All sections were projected onto plasterboards and then cut out by hand. The bar also provided the perfect backdrop for a blind date between Joaquín Phoenix and Olivia Wilde in the movie "Her" (2013).

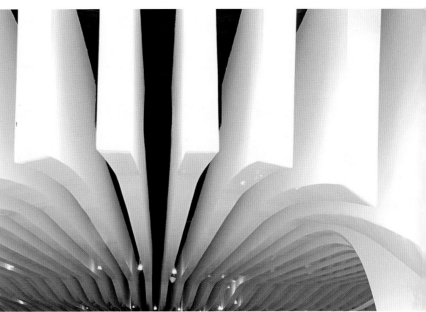

CARBON BAR AT PARK HOTEL

Central to the theme of the Park Hotel's bar Carbon is the creation of an oversized and highly faceted structure that boldly references a black diamond. The idea is abstracted by creating a dramatically faceted labyrinth that dynamically and unpredictably envelopes the entire space. Copper and dark champagne monotones are offset with surfaces in a bronze mirror. The furniture is angular in keeping with the esthetic of the outer shell. The walls' sharp edges are softened by luxurious padded fabric. Slivers of dimmable LED light emanate from translucent resin strip edging. The flooring is a seamless bronze vinyl, with the ceiling reflecting the same faceted shapes as the walls. The concept interprets the central theme of the hotel and the design brief – the Nizam of Hyderabad's jewels in a completely abstract and futuristic way.

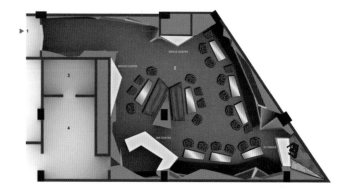

Architect | Khosla Associates
Location | Hyderabad, India
Size | 195 sqm
Completion | 2011
Type | bar

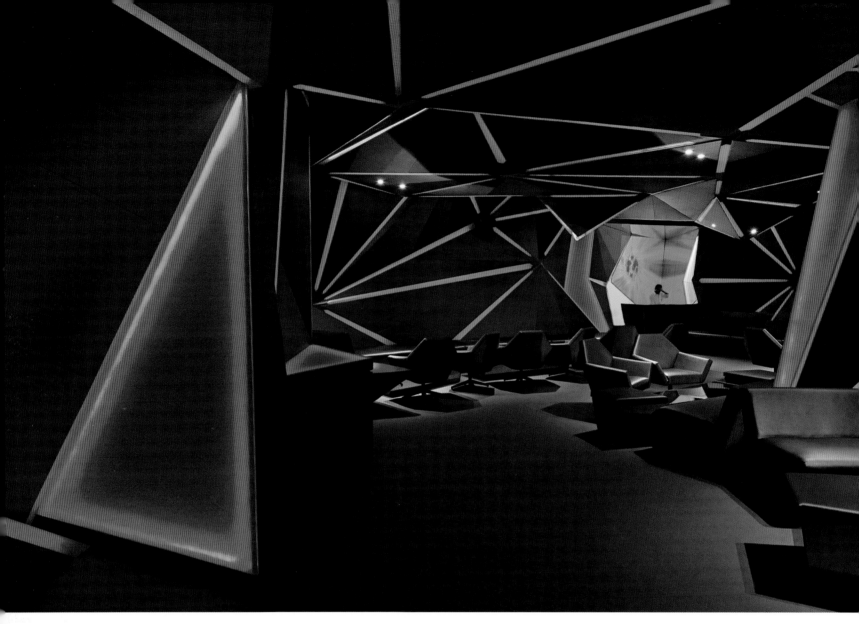

"Three o'clock is always too late or too early for anything you want to do." –
Jean-Paul Sartre, French philosopher

When the Gamsei in Munich's trendy Glockenbach district opened, "hyper-localism" crossed over to an area which had been reserved for restaurants. All the cocktail ingredients used in the Gamsei are either home-grown or provided by small entrepreneurs from the region; the design by Fabian A. Wagner from Buero Wagner and Andreas Kreft clearly continues this idea. Like the ingredients of the cocktails, the Buero Wagner drew on materials from the region to develop custom-fitted solutions in close cooperation with local craftsmen and manufacturers. Gamsei is a completely integrated concept that elevates the drinking of a cocktail to a new kind of experience.

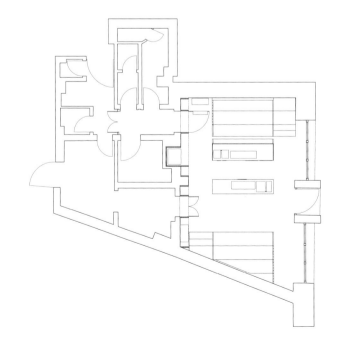

GAMSEI

Architect | Buero Wagner/Fabian A. Wagner with Andreas Kreft
Location | Buttermelcherstraße 9, Munich, Germany
Size | 40 sqm
Completion | 2013
Type | bar

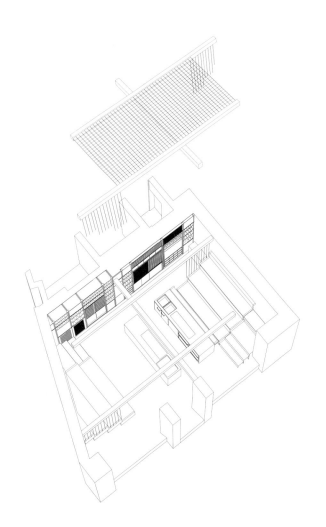

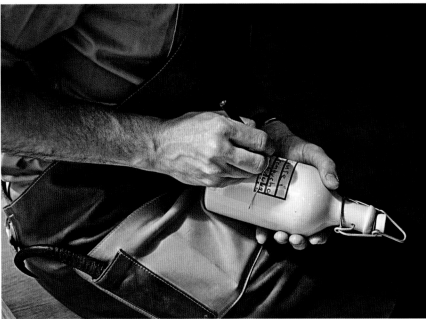

"The most contented fate is the release from doing and not doing" – Arthur Schopenhauer, German philosopher

PAKTA RESTAURANT

Architect | EL EQUIPO CREATIVO Oliver Franz Schmidt + Natali Canas del Pozo
Location | Calle Lleida, Barcelona, Spain
Size | 100 sqm
Completion | 2013
Type | restaurant & lounge

In the Quechua language of Peru "pakta" means "union"; in this case the union of two cultures and their respective cuisines. This is the idea behind the interior design created by El Equipo Creativo, with Japanese cuisine as the basis of the Nikkei gastronomy, but wrapped in Peruvian tastes, colors, traditions and ingredients. The basic elements of the restaurant, such as the bars, the kitchen and the furniture are designed with a clear reference to the architecture of the traditional Japanese taverns. The work areas are divided into three zones: in the entrance, the sake and pisco bar also acts as a filter between the interior and exterior. Facing outside, the bar becomes the façade and welcomes guests with a composition of faded colors, Japanese lamps, graphic elements and a small product display.

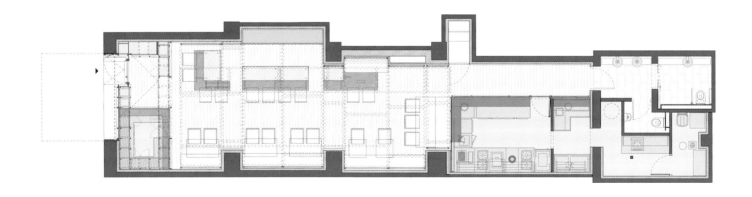

"What happens without taking a break cannot last."
– Ovid, Roman poet

Spanning 600 square meters at the top of the 36-floor ANA InterContinental Tokyo, MIXX by Curiosity is a playful exploration of light and shadows offering an atmospheric window over the city of Tokyo. A palette of neutral grey beige is contrasted with multilayered materials of washed wood, ray skins covering, hammered bronze and stone complemented by textured fabrics handcrafted by textile designer Reiko Sudo of Nuno. The space fuses traditional craftsmanship and Japanese art with modern design. Next to the open bar space is the main bar area. A signature 10-meter-long counter sets a bold tone, taking center stage against a backdrop of windows that reveal Mount Fuji by day and Tokyo's digital light show by night. Finally, there is the lounge. A white artwork of fabric hovering in the dark marks the entrance, leading to a central table and more intimate sofas tucked snugly into the zig-zag line of windows that surround the space. Cocooned by a series of vertical lights, the lighting dynamically cuts through the atmospheric dark space.

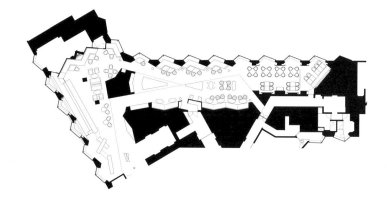

MIXX BAR & LOUNGE

Architect | GWENAEL NICOLAS, CURIOSITY
Location | ANA InterContinental Tokyo, Tokyo, Japan
Size | 600 sqm
Completion | 2010
Type | bar & lounge

"All cats are grey by night." – German proverb

MOJO CLUB

Two horizontal gates leading down to the interior provide entry to the newly opened Hamburg Mojo Club. Awaiting the visitors is a several floors high concert hall topped by a high vault where the organisation is concentrated. The design follows the character of the several floor-high concrete shell construction, oriented with its circular shape to a classical concert hall. A gallery surrounds the dance floor below in front of the stage where the music meets the guests. The interplay between the wood of the stage floor, the hall and rows of seating creates a resonant space. Acoustically adaptable wall facing made of perforated wood paneling with integrated lighting allows for alternating spatial situations.

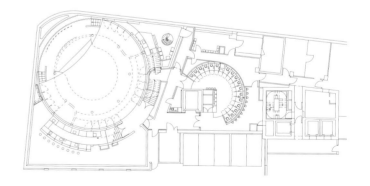

Architect | Thomas Baecker Bettina Kraus
Location | Reeperbahn 1, Hamburg, Germany
Size | 1,720 sqm
Completion | 2013
Type | club

"Music gives a soul to the universe, wings to the mind, flight to the imagination and life to everything." – Plato, Greek philosopher

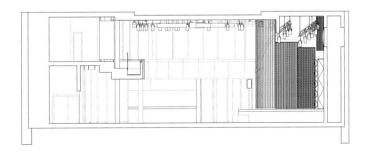

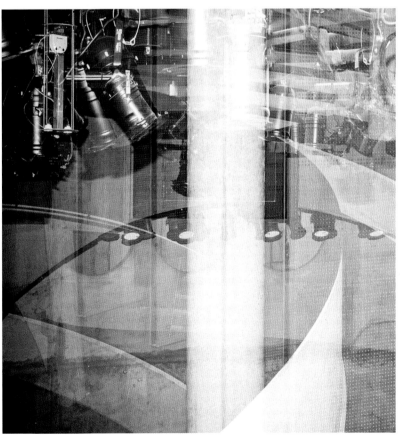

"Do it big, do it right, and do it with style." –
Fred Astaire, American dancer, actor and singer

64

HELIPORT VIP LOUNGE

This heliport located in Hong Kong's central district has long provided prestigious travel between Hong Kong and Macau. Two big challenges were turned by the designer into two key design elements: First, the angular shape of the envelop was wisely adopted by using groups of hexagonal zones linked to the centralized buffet counters, creating a geometric, manageable layout. Second, the low headroom under the steel beams and low structural soffit, were mitigated by three parabolic ceiling domes.

Interior designer | Mission & Associates Limited
Location | Inner Pier, Deck 6, 202 Connaught Road Central, Hong Kong
Size | 1,456 sqm
Completion | 2009
Type | lounge

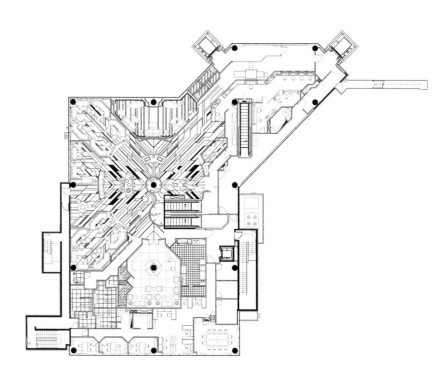

An old factory warehouse was stripped of its external walls to allow the insides to be infused with natural light. By doing so a view of the large trees along the road was created from its internal spaces, transforming them into a restaurant and a nightclub. The upper level houses a restaurant space and the lower level opening into an outdoor patio is a nightclub. The two levels are a complete contrast, with one dominated by steel and the other by wood, creating different experiences within the same space. Abstractly folded planes in metal encapsulate the entire lower level while undulating folded planes in strips of recycled wood constitute the upper level of Auriga. The abstraction of each space, with one merging into the other through the centrally located double-height volume, integrates them simultaneously.

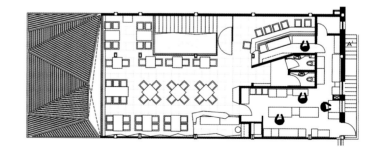

AURIGA

Architect | SANJAY PURI ARCHITECTS
Location | Mahalaxmi, Mumbai, India
Size | 390 sqm
Completion | 2013
Type | club & restaurant

"I love dance because it liberates people from the ponderousness of things." – Augustinus Aurelius, philosopher, church father and saint

Brinkworth created a sparse and unexpected backdrop for a unique dining experience, using steel, wire mesh, concrete, timber, and reeded glass to define the environment. An eclectic selection of light fixtures and customized furniture softens the otherwise brutal material palette. The site extends across two floors, with access to the raw and minimal bar downstairs through the ground floor restaurant. A custom-made metal mesh structure screens the traffic to the bar from the dining space and doubles up as a coat storage, while creating an acoustic buffer between the two spaces. The large windows of the corner site flood the restaurant with light in the daytime, while at night the windows reflect the sparkly effect of the interior lighting.

DABBOUS

Architect | Brinkworth
Location | 39 Whitfield St , London W1T 2SF, UK
Size | 207 sqm
Completion | 2012
Type | bar & restaurant

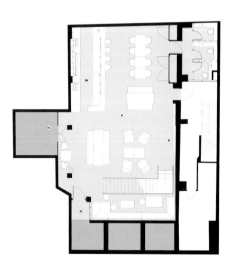

74

"One has to celebrate things as they come along."
– German proverb

GRAFFITI CAFÉ

Architect | STUDIO MODE
Location | 9000 Varna, Bulgaria
Size | 300 sqm
Completion | 2011
Type | bar & lounge

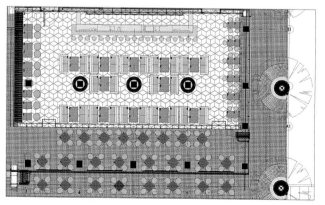

The interior works as a natural continuation of the architecture and is separated into two zones: the front zone was incorporated into the exterior creating public space and the feeling of a building console silhouette; the rear zone was separated by a floor and roof design that allowed reducing spatial depth while keeping the panorama. Studio Mode wanted an Escher-inspired space but had to deal with complex acoustic and ventilation issues. They created a unique concept that masters the space while satisfying all technological and functional requirements. The result is a trendy interior with a sufficient dose of artistry and a reference to the Gallery of Modern Art situated on the next level of the building.

"Enjoyment is just as important as work." –
Gotthold Ephraim Lessing, German writer

The assignment was to turn a parking garage into a restaurant and nightclub. After a research trip to Poland, including visits to old factories, the concept took shape and the restaurant was named Nazdrowje (Polish for "cheers"). The raw atmosphere of the space was kept and used as a base for the concept. Floors were made of concrete and cast benches were mounted directly onto the walls. A large fireplace in copper and a unique lighting arrangement was designed to give warmth to the industrial environment. The vintage pendant lamps from a factory in the Czech Republic together with the vintage Tolix chairs blends in well with the raw atmosphere. Frequently recurring materials include concrete, copper, steel and white tiles.

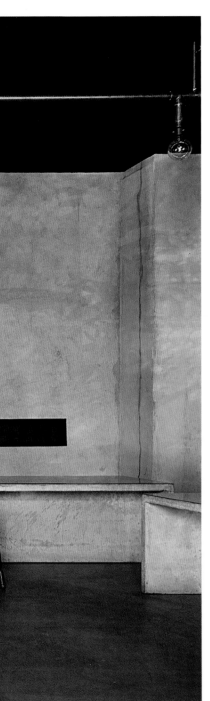

NAZDROWJE

Industrial charm in new surroundings. Rough materials and fine details determine the sensuality of this location.

Design | Richard Lindvall
Location | Edövagen 2, 13230 Saltsjö-Boo, Sweden
Size | 210 sqm
Completion | 2011
Type | bar & restaurant

ZENSE: THE REBIRTH

Don't call it a bar or restaurant... It is much more: A fascinating fusion of fashion, interior design, landscaping and architecture.

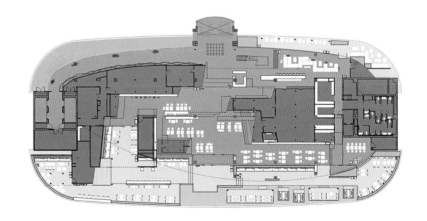

Architect | Department of ARCHITECTURE
Lighting designer | Accent Studio
Location | Centralworld Shopping Complex, Pathumwan, Bangkok
Size | 4,000 sqm
Completion | 2012
Type | bar & restaurant

After severe damages caused by riots in 2010, DEPT was called to give ZENSE another life after death. The designers decided to enhance their original spatial design with a more vibrant color scheme and stronger articulation. They continued their original approach of fusing four design disciplines: fashion design, interior design, landscape architecture, and architecture. To reflect the character of the project owner, ZEN Department Store, the dynamic world of fashion was introduced in the static domain of architecture, with the technique of pleating fabric into architectural elements and function. Pleating elements are found throughout the interior, from pleated stairs and railing, pleated seating, pleated performing stage, to pleated roofs over show kitchens.

85

RESTAURANT LOEWENECK

Architect | Dyer-Smith Frey
Location | Loewenstrasse 34, 8001 Zurich, Switzerland
Size | 93 sqm
Completion | 2014
Type | restaurant & bar

The spatial design reflects the concept of the kitchen: fresh and authentic. Unfinished wood, tin flashing, white tiles, exposed concrete walls and open ventilation ducts lend the room clear lines. Old joins up with new with the elegant ceiling lighting, industrial wall lamps and chairs by Manufaktur Horgenglarus, contributing idiosyncratic charm to the room. The Aztec pattern of the Dyer-Smith Frey custom-built bench provides the color element. The graphic counter made of unfinished wood in the middle of the room is also custom-built. The large windows and the marble pillars pick up design elements of the exterior façade.

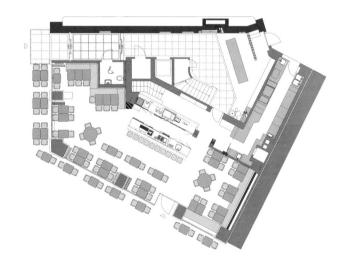

"A jovial dinner parties make for a regrettable morning after." – Martin Luther, German theologian and reformer

LIGHT CAVE

Modern architecture meets Japanese elegance.
A fairy-tale world composed of sculptural light objects – but not just for architecture aficionados.

Architect | Moriyuki Ochiai Architects
Location | Tokyo, Japan
Size | 96 sqm
Completion | 2014
Type | bar & restaurant

Moriyuki Ochiai Architects created the interior design for a restaurant and bar in a long and narrow cave-like setting where dynamic ridges and furrows form luminous vicissitudes that artfully create a space enfolded in a brilliant burst of illumination. Glimmering fragments of light adorn the area next to the entrance — like shards of ice or crystal — lending the space a serene atmosphere reminiscent of light on a cool winter day. Like living creatures freely roaming about, luminous aluminum waves whirl through the air and intertwine with the red timber lattice at the boundary of the back area facing large windows. The result is a space brimming with a feeling of lively motion. The characteristic creases of light at the front and back of the cave resonate with the shards of light, luminous aluminum and red timber lattice in their path, thereby bringing each microcosm into alignment and coalescing into a unique ensemble.

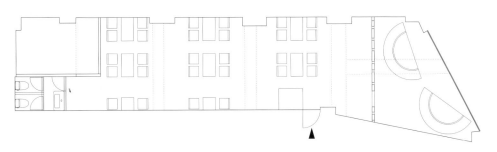

Architect | KAI Design
Wallpaper design, and graphics | Arm & Eye
Location | Birmingham, UK
Size | 550 sqm
Completion | 2012
Type | bar

The floor-to-ceiling botanical library is dimly lit with library lamps on long tables. Adjoining the library is a boardroom where the mythical character "Hettie" would gather her fellow professors and guests to discuss her findings. A secret doorway through a bookcase leads to Hettie's 'secret emporium'. Bespoke wallpaper flecked with gold leaf envelopes the room and gives it a dark and cosy feeling. Bell jars of potions and botanical oils surround the bar where elixirs are served to all of Hettie's guests. This project was awarded with Best Standalone Bar Design from the Restaurant and Bar Design Awards.

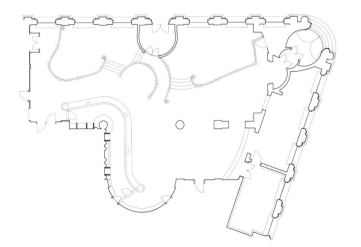

"We can't do anything against the night, but we can light a candle." – Franz von Assisi, Catholic friar and preacher

NIGHT FLIGHT

Architect | STUDIO MODE
Location | 1000 Sofia, Bulgaria
Size | 1,000 sqm
Completion | 2013
Type | club

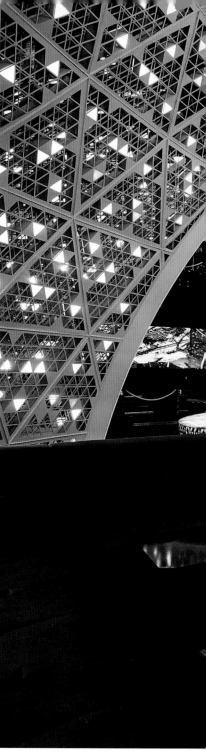

Night Flight is a live music club spread out over 1,000 square meters. Inspired by its name, the designers recreated the notion of a midnight walk or flight under a starry sky. The stage is situated in the center of the space in order to achieve 360° contact with the audience. The seating is arranged in three tiers and one balcony. The boudoir for the VIP tier overlooks the main hall. The designers set up the night scenery by using the quieting effect of sound insulation – adding extra depth to the walls and absorbing all light reflections. The glittering of stars is represented by a luminous web – a spherical surface that enhances the central perspective. Mirror reflections are used to multiply and modify the spatial proportions. Emphasizing detail, enriching it and pursuing the concept in depth resulted in a multilayer experience.

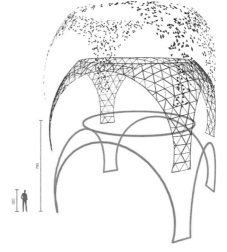

101

"Dance is a poem and every movement is a word."
— Mata Hari, Dutch dancer and spy

MOCHA MOJO

Mocha Mojo is a coffeehouse with 110 covers in Madras and space for coffee and conversations. The design refers to the 1970s mastery of "special" – furniture/wallpaper which in turn goes back to the early modernists' approach towards interiors: beauty through purity, reduction to functionalist objects, light on pure material, on pure color. Except in Mocha Mojo, old 1960s and 1970s qualities of "opulence" and "ornament" were reinfused into interiors resulting in spaces of great intensity, which was the goal for this project. Everything was generated in 3D and then built on site with a Lego-like construction.

104

Architect | Mancini Enterprises
Location | Adyar, Chennai, Tamil Nadu, India
Size | 325 sqm
Completion | 2009
Type | coffee bar

"Leisure seems to be the bearer of desire, true happiness and a blissful life." – Aristoteles, Greek philosopher

106

CLUB THE A

Art into music. Discover the many facetted jewel in
the heart of Gangnam.

Design firm Urbantainer has designed another jewel in Seoul's pulsating landscape. Situated in the heart of Gangnam, Club The A opened in June 2013. The club has been created following the designers' approach of closely interweaving design, culture and technology. The design concept employs an abstraction of the letter "A", expressed by the triangle. The three-sided polygon is not only the smallest design unit for colored patterns and sculptural installations, it also builds the foundation for the whole BI and visual identity system. Within the club, there is a "white corridor" which can be used for exhibitions or media art installations. This unusual space for a club adds another layer to an already rich sensual experience. Special attention was paid to the mobile DJ booth which is made of triangles with an integrated custom-made LED system to provide an iconic glow.

Architect | URBANTAINER
Location | B1/B2F Artnouveau City, 701-1 Yeoksam-dong, Kangnam-gu, Seoul, South Korea
Size | 1,380 sqm
Completion | 2013
Type | club

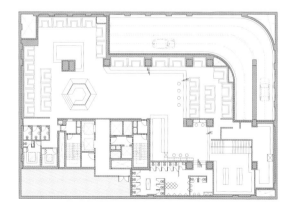
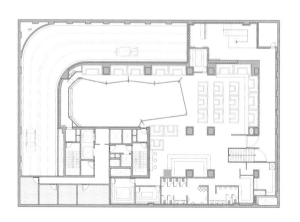

A legendary Berlin-Kreuzberg bar rises again. The rambling floor plan creates an atmosphere reminiscent of the past and accented with new elements of design. The play with disconnects is as exciting as in the district itself: a 1950s wooden rod wall and Chesterfield sofa paired off against a concrete fireplace and cement tiles; a buffet made of historic Berlin hotel mirrors and a counter made of Berlin stove tiles merging into leather blinds congregate beneath New York tin ceiling tiles. It is the contrast-rich use of materials and light, history and design, which gives the bar its atmosphere.

112

DIE BAR

Architect | unit-berlin
Location | Skalitzer Straße 64, Berlin, Germany
Size | 170 sqm
Completion | 2013
Type | bar

"Any man who eats dessert is not drinking enough."
– Ernest Hemingway, American author

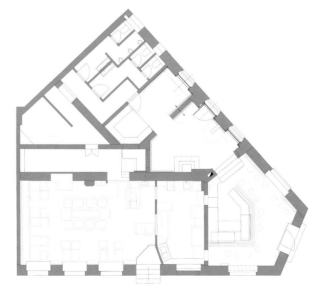

114

The Lesinska Concept presents Cafe Wedel as a venture into a chocolate wonderland, completed for the famous Polish confectionery company. The different seating spaces are defined by bold pieces of furniture are set against delicate gold finishings. Glittering surfaces and pastel colors enhance these juxtapositions, with traditional materials such as maple wood, Carrera marble and brass conveying durability and timelessness. The 'chocolate ceiling' reminiscent of dripping chocolate was paired with a smooth ceiling surface illuminated by LEDs and a smooth white surface in parts of the lobby.

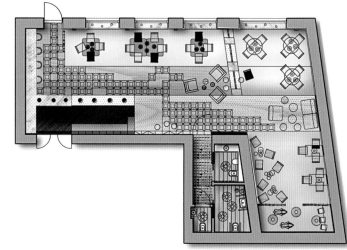

CAFE WEDEL

Architect | LESINSKA CONCEPT
Location | Poland
Size | 160 sqm
Completion | 2013
Type | bar

"Without the class of idlers people would be
barbarians today." –
Bertrand Russell, British philosopher

Inspired by the dynamic carving of skis through snow, the W Verbier hotel brings an indelible, distinct New York City glamour to the ski resort in the Swiss Alps. The design features smooth lines that carve through the spaces, a movement the skis leave in the mountains Verbier is so famous for. In the W Livingroom a wooden block with carved out seating elements and fireplaces offers a spectacular view down the valley. As a contrast, a carved light feature made of different types of wood is suspended above it, following its footprint. The bar is formed by a giant, carved 'ice rock' made of glass where guests come to meet and mingle. Guests can dance the night away at the CARVE bar which is hidden in the mountain and can only be accessed by entering a red tunnel through the giant staircase. The giant staircase is situated next to the living room in one of the glass atriums connecting the four chalet buildings.

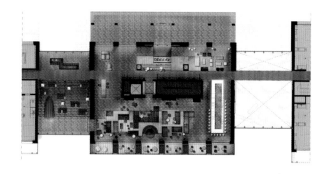

W VERBIER

Architect | concrete architectural associates
Location | Rue de Médran 70, Verbier, Switzerland
Size | 14,200 sqm
Completion | 2013
Type | lounge & bar

"The end of labor is to gain leisure." –
Aristotle, Greek philosopher

BUSINESS CLUB ALLIANZ ARENA

Architect | CBA Clemens Bachmann Architekten
Client | Allianz Arena München Stadion GmbH
Location | Werner-Heisenberg-Allee 25, Munich, Germany
Size | 3,500 sqm
Completion | 2013
Type | club & restaurant

"Everything in the world is folly, except amusement."
– Frederick the Great, Prussian king

The project includes the redesign of the business club in the Allianz Arena, the home of FC Bayern München. The area is the heart of the stadium with a total floor area of 3,500 square meters and a maximum capacity of 2,200 guests. The original big food counters where replaced by smaller units which resemble little market stalls. The counters were faced with waved wood panels, suggesting movement and emotion. The different sizes and curves of the waves intersect horizontally, creating a strong 3D effect. The smooth light brown color provides a modest background for the food and beverages. The Rolf Benz furniture completes the business club concept, achieving a new standard in hospitality and interior design for stadiums.

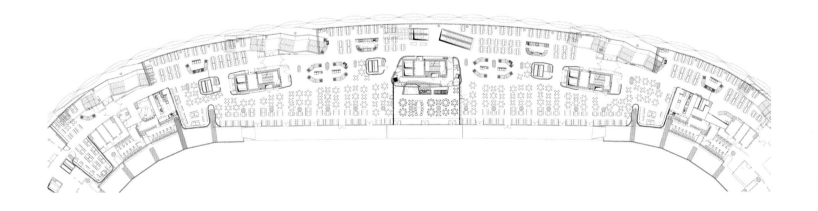

127

EL FABULOSO

Located in one of the busiest streets of the city of Bogotá, El Fabuloso (The Fabu-lous) is a high-end bar and restaurant with capacity for about 500 people. The space that is enveloped by a wood timber tissue is designed as an acoustic element. The project stems from the idea of the experience and atmosphere of a picnic, the idea of celebrating the day, to enjoy a good sunset. The site is intended as a basket contain-ing different experiences; the tissue is opened and closed depending on the acoustics and the different views of the city from within. All the interiors are made of three basic raw materials: wood, metal and concrete. The place has several terraces where the gardens and water create a relaxing atmosphere to see the city and the different façades of the project.

Architect | MEMA arquitectos
Interior designer | MEMA arquitectos + Colette Studio
Location | Calle 85 n.º 14 - 05. Piso 7. Bogotá, Colombia
Size | 420 sqm
Completion | 2013
Type | bar & restaurant

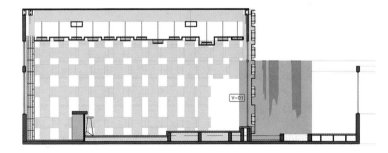

129

"There are two types of human being: One thinks, the other amuses himself." – Montesquieu, French political philosopher

CRONUS PRIVATE BAR
AND LOUNGE

The charm of days gone by in a ballet of ancient elegance. For members only!

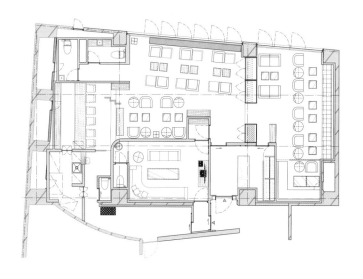

Architect | Doyle Collection
Location | Nishiazabu, Minato-ku, Tokyo, Japan
Size | 150 sqm
Completion | 2012
Type | bar & lounge

This members' bar and lounge targets those who are keen on the stylish Tokyo night life. By stepping into the reception hall warm lights illuminate the patrons. They find themselves reflected in the black-frame-mirrored wall surface. A walk through this hall changes the customers' moods. Bookshelves occupying the walls look like a luxurious study room in the hotel lounge. In order to contrast the artifacts (books), the designers used natural rock as reliefs that provide extraordinary impressions. The luxurious color they chose, champagne gold, makes for a good balance. A custom-made wine cellar divides the spacious room. Cronus was awarded with the Best Bar in Asia award from the 2013 Restaurant and Bar Design Awards.

135

L'OSTERIA BIKINI BERLIN

Interior designer | DiPPOLD Innenarchitektur
Location | Budapester Straße 28–50, 10787 Berlin, Germany
Size | 560 sqm
Completion | 2014
Type | bar & restaurant

"Idleness is fatal only to the mediocre." –
Albert Camus, French author.

The first L'Osteria in the capital celebrates its opening in the Bikini Haus. On the ground floor of the new annex you will find 360 square meters of space for guests and a terrace with an outstanding view of the Gedächtniskirche. The vibrant ambience is created by the open kitchen, deftly composed by Dippold Innenarchitektur. The décor is a mixture of lovingly selected unique pieces with furniture especially designed for the location. The long bar invites to linger and watch. One of the highlights is the vintage lighting concept with the "Cucina" lettering. Lattice windows in connection with colored subway tiles import a great atmosphere to the glazed building. A pulsating location which deliberately provokes makes every visit memorable.

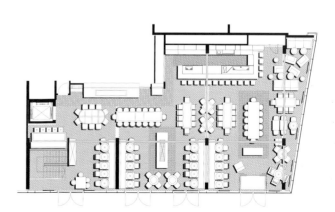

DAS STUE

Tradition allies with the modern. The sublime and subdued charisma lends this location its special character.

Architect | Axthelm Architekten
Interior designer | Patricia Urquiola
Location | Drakestraße 1, 10787 Berlin, Germany
Size | 7,890 sqm
Completion | 2012
Type | bar, lounge & restaurant

Located in the area of Berlin Tiergarten Das Stue presents itself as a thrilling combination of a memorial, built by J.E. Schaudt in 1940 as a Danish legation, with new sculptural construction. The historical building was completely rearranged and added with an new modern sculptural building by Axthelm Architekten. Das Stue's unique heritage is reflected in its name, the Danish term for "living room". The central entrance hall recreates the heart of the old building. The natural stone façade of the historical building is answered by the photo concrete façade of the new building. A floral pattern announces the softer materials with the same design in the inner areas of the hotel. The cubature of the supplementary new building was designed in order to illuminate the atrium with southern light so that all rooms on the back side of the old building have views into the surrounding compounds of the Berlin Zoo. Patricia Urquiola, Spanish architect and designer, brings her signature sleek and elegant touch to the hotel's interiors.

PINTXOS

Tapas beneath the crowns of trees in a magical world. Which is also Kuwait.

Architect | PS STUDIO
Location | Al Seif Strip, Kuwait City, Kuwait
Size | 170 sqm
Completion | 2013
Type | bar

Pintxos is a highly sensual and immersive environment with mysterious lighting, tactile richness and undulating soft forms. The space is divided by three elevated seating platforms, each finished with a single material such as steel, wood and carpet. The ceiling is a suspended terrain of nearly two thousand felt cones which were developed to provide lighting, acoustical absorption and spatial definition. The ceiling undulating surface defines the seating spaces, booths and lounge and the passages in between. The furniture made of soft materials like felt, wool and leather, features curvilinear forms to complement the ceiling topography. The bar wall, a perforated surface of basalt and felt, provides backlight.

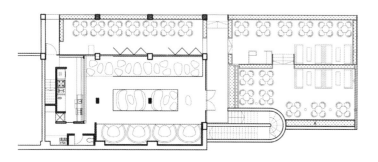

This bar in the attic of a newly rebuilt house in Minsk Old Town stands out as an example of honest use of raw materials. The original brickwork is left bare, with the bar counter executed in the same brick. Two main features organize the space. First, it is a multifunctional structure in pine boards, spanning the entire space, with a bar, lamp, a shelf and a coat rack. Taken together, it highlights the space as an archetypal attic. Second, it is a soft seating structure occupying an otherwise unusable space found under a low ceiling. The dividing elements 'mirror' the sloped ceiling, completing the space. Smaller objects of the interior, new and old, have been carefully collected by the architects from different epochs and sources around the globe.

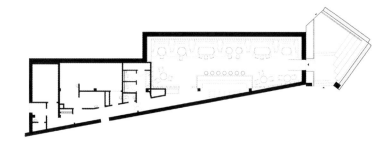

ATTIC BAR

Design | Inblum Architects
Location | Zibickaia 9, Minsk, Belarus
Size | 131 sqm
Completion | 2013
Type | bar

"Never refuse to do a kindness unless the act
would work great injury to yourself, and never refuse
to take a drink – under any circumstances."
– Mark Twain, American author

BAR SAINT JEAN

Architect | Thilo Reich
Location | Steinstraße 21, 10119 Berlin, Germany
Size | 85 sqm
Completion | 2013
Type | bar

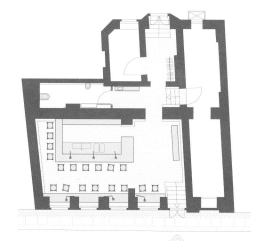

The young French owner just moved from Paris to Berlin to start his own business: a little bar with a French touch. A palette of muted grays, greens, and browns defines the conspiratorial air of the bar. Dark green painted walls and anthracite oak floorboards create a dim and cosy atmosphere. A large, generously proportioned bar in the center allows most of the guests to gather around the barman. The counter and the window sill are made of ancient ship planks, which, before being stripped of tar, had been used as a fence on a farm in France. The artistic assemblage lends the space a feeling of rustic charm. Industrial black bar stools and French lamps with rusty lampshades generate contrasts that are repeated by other reused rusty objects hanging under indirect illumination on the walls.

153

"Never sit a table when you can stand at the bar."
– Ernest Hemingway, American author

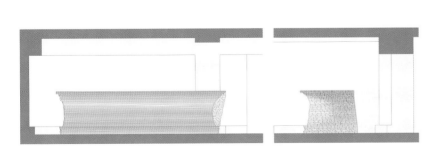

Interior designer | Corvin Cristian in collaboration with Vlad Vieru
Size | 200 sqm
Location | Smardan Street, Bucharest, Romania
Completion | 2012
Type | bar & restaurant

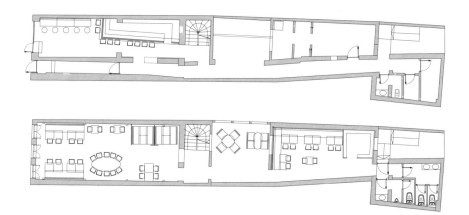

BON is a French restaurant on Smardan Street, in the historical center of Bucharest, Romania. Over 200 reclaimed doors, windows and blinds were used as wall paneling. Carefully placed light sources add to the theatrical yet cozy atmosphere. Some of the doors were rescued from building sites – hence the graffiti and the extreme wear some of them display. Corvin Cristian left most of the doors as found while only the shades of a few were altered to meet the discreet three tone color scheme (white, blue, red). The designer's approach is also an attempt to keep some memories of the disappearing past of Central Bucharest.

"There can't be good living where there is not good drinking." – Benjamin Franklin, American scientist and statesman

BAR FURCO

Architect | Zébulon Perron
Size | 278 sqm
Location | Montreal, Québec, Canada
Completion | 2013
Type | bar

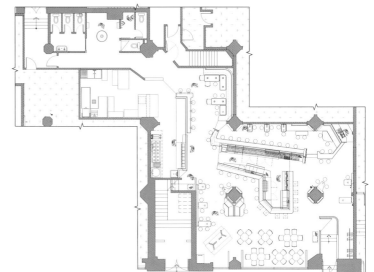

In this abandoned fur warehouse that used to house the Canadian Fur Company (Fur + Company = Furco) this new bar has taken up residence. In order to create the specific feel that the designers of Zébulon Perron wanted for this project they selectively stripped the walls, columns and ceilings. As a counterpoint to these rough surfaces the original mouldings were restored to their former glory. At Furco, rough concrete is omnipresent and contrasts with the large gleaming brass bar that dominates the center of the 3,000-square-feet space. The combination of these elements aims for a laid back and chic look. A monumental light fixture was also built specifically for this project. Snaking from the entrance, a sinuous rail supports custom lamps, suggesting a path that leads to a fountain installed in a common space outside the bathrooms.

162

"The problem with the world is that everyone is a few drinks behind." –
Humphrey Bogart, American actor

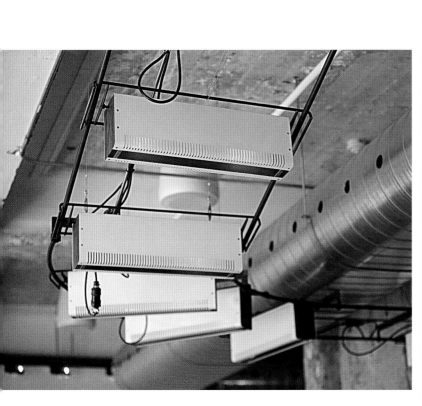

Don Café House is the first concept introduced by the Don Café company in Kosova. By studying and researching Don Café, Innarch came up with a unique visual concept which distinguishes it from traditional coffee bars by giving it a modern image. A sack filled with coffee beans is the inspiration for the design. The walls of the bar are organically shaped and colored like a coffee sack made of plywood, with the pillars covered with textile coffee sacks. Tables and chandeliers represent the coffee beans lined up asymmetrically in order to generate the impression of being inside a coffee sack. The bar shape also plays an important role by generating diversities in the types of coffees on the menu.

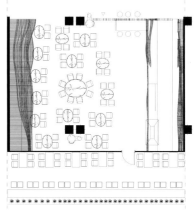

DON CAFÉ HOUSE

Architect | INNARCH Arch. Visar GECI
Location | shopping center Albi Mall, Prishtina, Republic of Kosova
Size | 130 sqm
Completion | 2013
Type | café & lounge

"There are more important things in life than constantly increasing its speed." – Mahatma Gandhi, Indian independence movement leader.

167

BURJ EL HAMAM
RESTAURANT

Architect | Galal Mahmoud / GM Architects
Location | Doha, Qatar
Size | 300 sqm
Completion | 2008
Type | restaurant & bar

In a prime location in The Pearl Doha, Burj el Hamam was built to reflect the Lebanese taste for tradition. Galal Mahmoud of GM Architects has created an interior décor with an atmosphere that is both classic and contemporary. Inspired by traditional 19th century Beirut palaces, the interior has a muted color palette ranging from dusty pink to light grey, producing a sense of opulence and luxury. Imposing glistening gold columns and impressive chandeliers decorate the restaurant's capacious dining area, with large windows that take advantage of its prime waterfront location. Built originally as a two-story space, the upper floor was removed to gain dramatic height and outfitted with six two-meter-high glass chandeliers that were custom-designed in Italy, inspired by the Ottoman era, which influenced some Lebanese architecture. Subtle blends of luxurious Middle Eastern details contrast with contemporary minimalism.

169

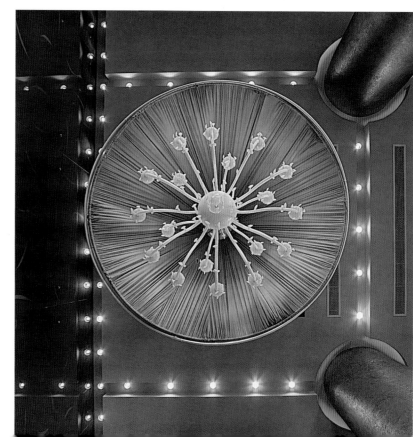

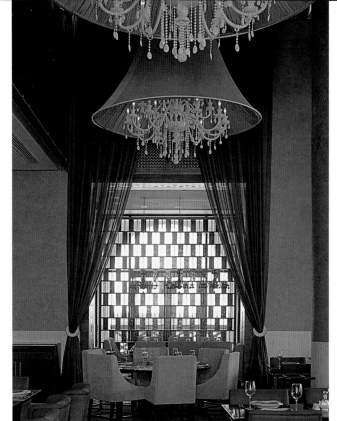

"Doesn't everything which thrill us bear the color of night?" – Novalis, German poet

EVENT LOUNGE
AT BEISHEIM CENTER

Architect | de Winder
Size | 650 sqm
Location | Berliner Freiheit 2, 10785 Berlin, Germany
Completion | 2009
Type | lounge & event location

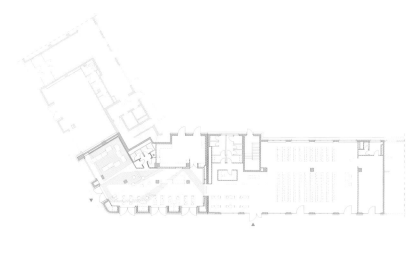

A high-quality event location has been created in the Berlin Beisheim Center. The white cube studio can be adapted depending on the event, with interior technology controlled via smartphone using the revolutionary Web 2.0 technology. On the way to the washrooms the adjustable LED light in the RGB color zone creates optical irritation. The adjacent salon designed as a lounge features an ultra-modern catering kitchen with mobile cooking units for live preparation. A variously colored, luminous, three-dimensional graphic concept winds through the space, beginning in the floor as stripes, leading through cut-outs in the wall to join up with the coved ceiling lighting.

"Let us read, and let us dance; these two amuse-
ments will never do any harm to the world."
– Voltaire, French writer

THE CONGA ROOM

Pure Latin-American grit. A special zest for life and
a firework of the senses in Downtown LA.

Architect | Belzberg Architects
Location | L.A. Live, Los Angeles, California, USA
Size | 1,300 sqm
Completion | 2008
Type | club & restaurant

The Conga Room, in its new location at L.A. Live in downtown Los Angeles, is the city's premier Latin nightclub. The space features today's hottest Latin performers in 14,000 square feet of live venue space, which includes a restaurant, three bars, patio seating, and a VIP lounge and private room. In addition, the club hosts LA TV and world-renowned DJs adjacent to the stage and above the crowd, adding even more excitement to the ambiance. The club aims to be true to the energy of the Latin community, to pay homage to its roots and rich history, while infusing it with the fervent Los Angeles modern lifestyle.

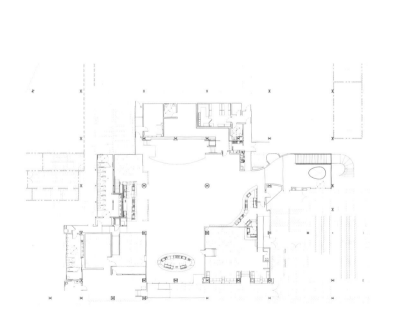

TWISTER

Interior designer | Architectural workshop SERGEY MAKHNO
Size | 421 sqm
Location | Kiev, Ukraine
Type | restaurant & bar

The contrast and contradiction of this restaurant's interior is not a chaotic eclecticism, but a conceptual and well thought-out design with a distinct style and the designer's vision of usual things. The design of the 250-square-meter restaurant emphasizes the 'flavor' of this particular place, where visitors are offered courses of modern molecular cuisine. Natural materials in the design, like wood, stone and metal, are used to create a feeling of ease and freedom from routine, with natural colors to bring a sense of calmness and security.

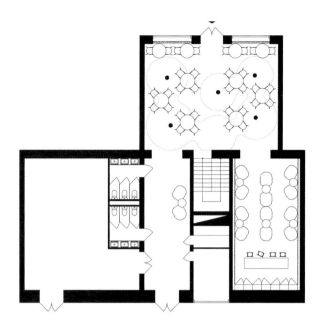
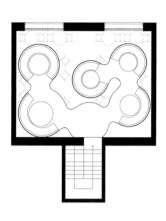

"There can be nothing more frequent than an occasional drink." –
Oscar Wilde, Irish writer and poet

GOLDENER PUDEL

Take a building from the 1950s, remodel it and add a touch of trash... and voila! An authentic urban site for nothing less than lingering is born.

Unconventional, young, authentic, and with a touch of 'trash' were the parameters specified by the sponsor. A budget of under 700 Euro per square meter was available for the project. The locality is located in a no-nonsense, sober building from the 1950s. A room height of just under 3.70 meters was a plus. The existing Odenwald dropped ceiling was removed to expose the cement surface underneath it. That was exactly what lends this space the 'trashy' and unusual character the sponsor was looking for. Clear lines, unified, smooth surfaces and the modern and the antiquated emerged from the exciting contrast between loft and a comfortable atmosphere. A locality was created which shows how life is lived in Nuremberg: with both feet on the ground, and venturesome, tolerant, honest and authentic.

Architect & interior designer | Gerhard Wittl
Interior design | roomcode
Location | Grasersgasse 15, Nuremberg, Germany
Size | 220 sqm
Completion | 2013
Type | bar

PIECE OF PARADISE

Architect | STUDIO MODE
Location | 1000 Sofia, Bulgaria
Type | bar & restaurant

The design concept was created in relation to the distinctive shape of the space – an irregular hexagon. The designers of Studio Mode ironed out the disordered figure to achieve a regular one and then applied a general mathematical correlation between all interior elements. The key to the task was structural combinatorics and work with the proportions and scale of a geometric shape. In order to achieve the balance of sensations needed, the designers chose a contrast of natural and 'warm', and synthetic and 'cold' materials. Drawing design inspiration from nature and the use of a simple geometric shape, they created the "honeycomb" motif.

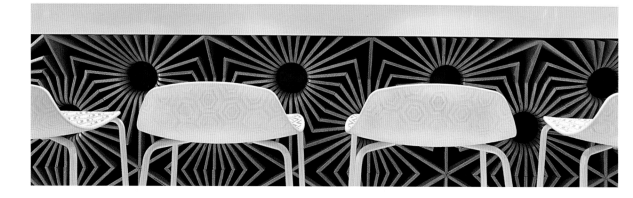

"I have Social Disease. I have to go out every night. If I stay home one night I start spreading rumors to my dogs." – Andy Warhol, American artist

GEKKOS

The bar is located on the ground floor of the Hilton Hotel in Frankfurt. It is a cross between a classical hotel and a scene bar, where international hotel guests rub shoulders with the Frankfurters. At night, the bar turns into a club. Due to the selection of dark colors and the mood of the light the bar has a secretive and intimate atmosphere. The name of Gekkos is inspired by the main character in the film Wallstreet. The room is divided in three zones: the 10-meter-long bar area with DJ console, the raised seating area and the two VIP niches. The bar counter reminds one of a gold credit card and is emphasized by four prominent candelabras. The two VIP niches are upholstered in dark blue satin and can be closed with a curtain like a cocoon.

Architect | Rosen Architekten
Size | 154 sqm
Location | Hochstraße 4, 60313 Frankfurt, Germany
Completion | 2010
Type | bar & club

"Always remember, that I have taken more out of alcohol than alcohol has taken out of me." – Winston Churchill, British statesman

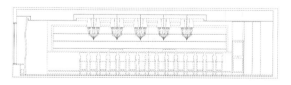

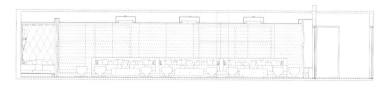

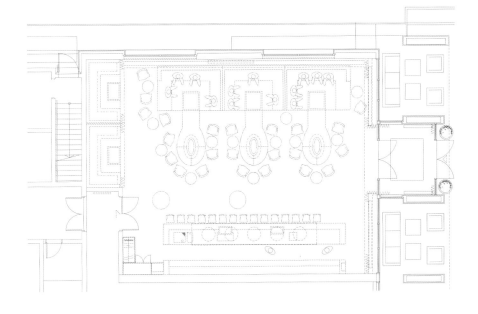

GENERATOR BARCELONA

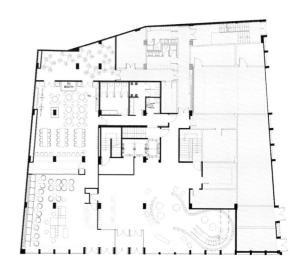

Architect | Ibinser
Designer | DesignAgency
Location | 5–7 Carre Coresega, Barcelona, Spain
Size | 364 sqm
Completion | 2013
Type | hotel, hostel, bar & lounge

As the flagship location for Generator, a global hostel chain with a mission to provide fun and affordable accommodation, Generator Barcelona used the opportunity to create fantastic, lively social spaces for a variety of uses. The design is grounded by a desire to move guests out of their rooms and into the hostel's playful common areas to mix and mingle. Local emerging artists were commissioned to create custom signature installations inspired by the neighborhood's annual street festival, the Festa Major de Gracia. The energy and vibrancy of the lobby and common areas set the tone for the Generator experience. A far cry from a typical hostel, Generator Barcelona captures the best of its host city and puts it on display.

"No one looks back on their life and remembers the nights they had plenty of sleep." – Unknown

PRESS CLUB

Totally Napa style: Warm materials and colors mixed with industry charm create perfect harmony.

Press Club's design is influenced by the Napa region's unique blend of industry and natural beauty. This urban tasting room brings the casual sophistication of a wine country experience to San Francisco, with eight small-production California wineries offering an array of vintages to sample or purchase. The entryway features a shop with rare wine libraries and current releases from each winery. The subterranean level includes bars maintained by each winery, lounge areas, a central bar and a private event room. The industrial and organic accent is emphasized in the pattern of four-inch American Black walnut planking, juxtaposed with the imprinting of board-formed cement plaster. Sapwood underscores this patterning.

Architect & interior designer | BCV Architects
Location | 20 Yerba Buena Lane, San Francisco, CA 94103, USA
Size | 762 sqm
Completion | 2008
Type | bar

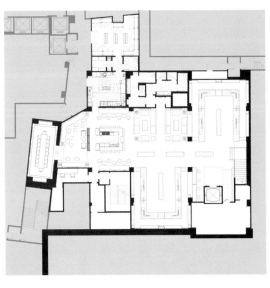

.HBC RESTAURANT & BAR &
JWD MOBILE VERSION

Architect | unit-berlin
Location | Karl-Liebknecht-Straße 9, 10178 Berlin, Germany
Size | 1,400 qm / 800 sqm
Completion | 2010 / 2013
Type | restaurant & bar

The reinventing of the restaurant and bar in the former Hungarian Cultural Institute at Alexanderplatz in Berlin boasts a unique approach to the location's history and architecture. unit-berlin was given the task of completely redesigning the dining area, bar and 'tower room'. This resulted in a design of stark contrasts and a very special atmosphere, typical of contemporary Berlin. Particularly prominent are the custom-made concrete-globe lamps. Referring to the .HBC, unit-berlin also developed a mobile version, the "JWD" (short for 'janzweitdraussen', or way-far-away), that transports the spirit of this location to other places and leaves subtle traces like the concrete/glass luster built by the guests during the music festival BLN+ in Lille.

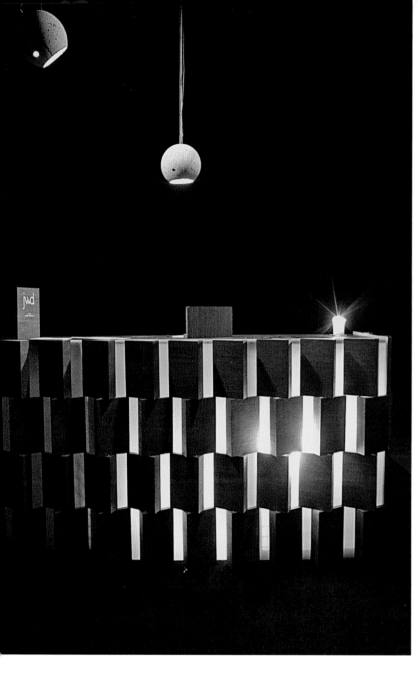

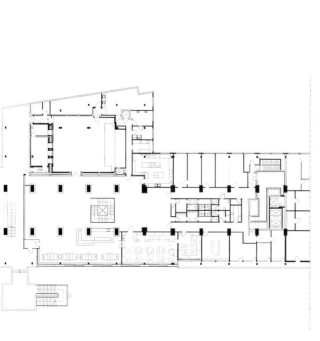

"Only change is positive. Constant daylight is wearisome." – Wilhelm von Humboldt, German statesman

The form of this venue for music lovers on one of Bangalore's prime streets draws inspiration from traditional barn architecture with its voluminous interior shell and an overriding gable roof. Various levels within a larger volume interact seamlessly with one another, while freeing sight lines from the stage at one end and the DJ booth on the other. The rear stage wall is stacked with logs to form a rich textural backdrop which cleverly references the firewood stacked in barns. The degree of customization extends to the furniture design, the light fixtures, and various other design details. The material palette is a mix of oak, olive colored structural steel, unfinished mild steel and distressed white brick. The dramatic interior volume of the building steps out into a calm and intimate courtyard open to the sky with its own bar for those seeking respite from the audio levels inside.

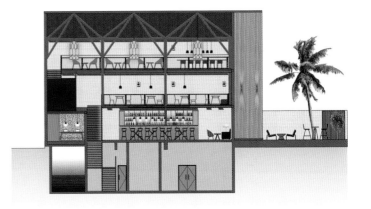

LOFT 38

Architect and interior designer | Khosla Associates
Location | Bangalore, Karnataka, India
Size | 775 sqm
Completion | 2013
Type | bar, club & restaurant

"We should consider every day lost when we have not danced at least once." –
Friedrich Nietzsche, German philosopher

LIEBHART

Architect | GIORGIO GULLOTTA ARCHITEKTEN
Size | 195 sqm
Location | Thaliastraße 63, 1160 Vienna, Austria
Completion | 2013
Type | bar & restaurant

"A drunken man's words are a sober man's thoughts."
– Old adage

New, young, fresh, traditional. A Viennese inn, café, restaurant, beer pub and bar in one. Variable seating arrangements and clever structuring of the space provide cheerful and comfortable flair. Finely finished surfaces and a modern, graphic form language transmit a modern spirit. For instance, the original bulky concrete counter was sand-blasted and roughened. Instead of the typical paneling, conically shaped wood pieces wrap the walls. Custom-made items made of wood with a love for detail and design pieces by Piet Hein Eek, Tom Dixon and Louis Poulsen provide the visual and haptic proof of honest materials.

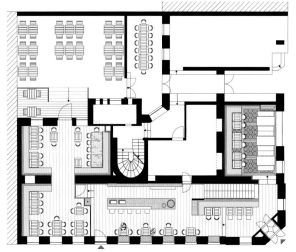

The renovation of the main floor living room, bar and restaurant was conceived around a "Sonic Lodge" which seeks to illuminate juxtapositions found in the history and futuristic aspirations of Seattle and the Great Northwest. The design invokes the interplay between past, present and future. Structural columns 36-inches in diameter are located throughout the interior. To create connectivity between spaces, these columns were masked with stacked modular elements responding to local site conditions. These lodge poles define the space, rhythmically employing the columns as a composition of new 20-foot tall interior pilings. The lodge poles are a new take on the wharf pilings, log structures and totems from the area.

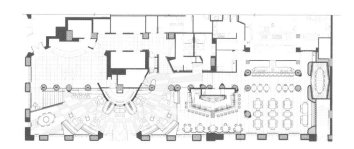

THE W SEATTLE

Architect | Skylab Architecture
Location | 1112 Fourth Avenue, Seattle, WA, USA
Size | 498 sqm
Completion | 2012
Type | bar, lounge & restaurant

"I often think that the night is more alive and more richly colored than the day." – Vincent van Gogh, Dutch painter

CLUB OCTAGON

Experience the power of the Octagon. A magic combination of club, lounge and restaurant as a very special location for entertainment.

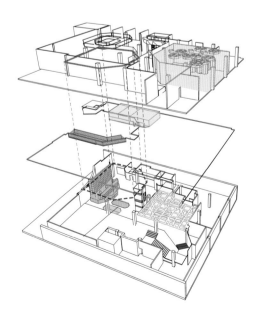

220

Architect | URBANTAINER
Location | B1/B2F 152 New Hilltop Hotel, Nonhyun-dong, Kangnam-gu, Seoul, South Korea
Size | 2,600 sqm
Completion | 2011
Type | club, lounge & restaurant

Club Octagon answers the client's request to renovate 2,640 square meters over two levels of run-down hotel basement to create a high tech auditorium, club, lounge and restaurant that puts music and people's experience first. Urbantainer developed a new type of multi-space for entertainment, socializing and subculture that was lacking in the South Korean market. Conceptually, every detail of Club Octagon works with the octagonal form from the corporate identity, including the layout, 4D media lighting, modular seating and even the ice buckets in each of the VIP rooms.

221

RADEGAST BEER PUB ATLANTIC

The Radegast Beer Pub promotes the Czech beer Radegast. It has a modern interior concept while still using traditional materials and old technologies in order to recreate the coziness of old pubs. The Czech porcelain ("Cibulák") is the inspiration behind the blue color and geometric ornamentation on the walls and ceiling. Free standing furniture is made of oak wood. Portals and railings are made of black steel and copper. Lighting is from the ARBO collection, which was designed by IO Studio.

Architect | Luka Križek, IO Studio
Location | Královická 300/6, Brandýs nad Labem 250 01, Czech Republic
Size | 150 sqm
Completion | 2013
Type | bar

"When I drink, I think; and when I think, I drink." – Francois Rabelais, French writer

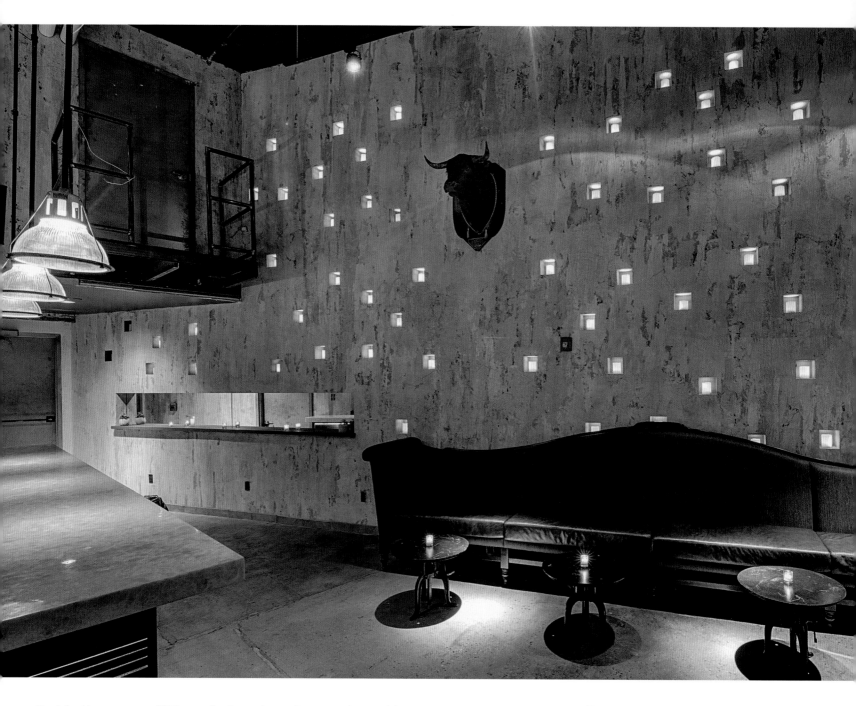

Toro's backbar serves as a VIP lounge for those who aren't quite ready to end their night after dinner. The design is a continuation of the restaurant's industrial elegance, boasting rich leather banquettes and a real ivy covered wall. The concrete floor is original, complimented by a white Carrara marble bar top, and blackened steel bar face. The exposed brick and warehouse pendants top off the raw industrial feeling of the space and the mosaic tile floor around the seating area brings in an air of Spanish elegance.

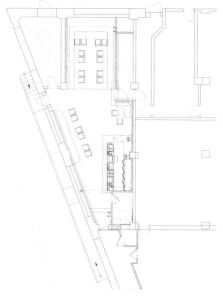

BACKBAR

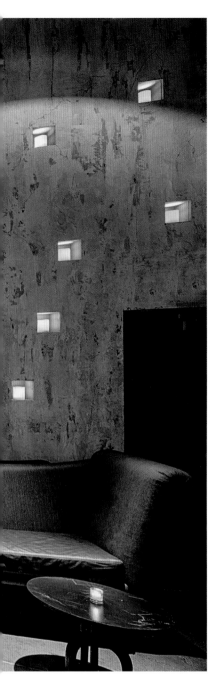

Architect | New World Design Builders
Location | 85 10th Avenue, New York City, NY, USA
Completion | 2013
Type | bar & lounge

"In victory, you deserve Champagne. In defeat you need it." –
Napoleon Bonaparte, French emperor

The Ikibana restaurant offers a fusion of Japanese and Brazilian gastronomies, two cultures that seem so antagonistic: the one quiet and minimalist, the other exuberant and bustling. Because of the importance of landscape in both cultures, that element is emphasized in a design of space that creates an artificial landscape. On the one hand Brazil represents an extraordinary lush landscape, with Brazilian lifestyle absorbing and reflecting this voluptuousness, always cheerful and full of color. On the other, traditional Japanese paintings, as well as the visual and dramatic arts, are full of references to their landscape. The art of flower arrangement known as Ikebana is one of the examples of this respect for nature deeply rooted in Japanese culture, giving its name to the restaurant and inspiration to its design.

IKIBANA PARAL.LEL

Free as a bird. Nest-like structures create a playful
yet stylish atmosphere for the Nipo-Brazilian restaurant experience.

Architect | EL EQUIPO CREATIVO Oliver Franz Schmidt + Natali Canas del Pozo
Location | Av. Paralelo 148 Barcelona, Spain
Size | 250 sqm
Completion | 2012
Type | restaurant & lounge

235

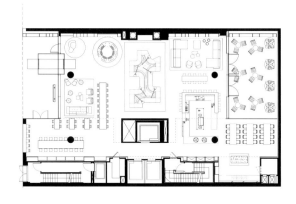

Architect | concrete architectural associates
Location | 218 West 50th Street, New York City, USA
Size | 500 sqm
Completion | 2014
Type | bar & lounge

The citizenM hotel designed by concrete is making its debut in the United States with its first skyscraper in the heart of New York City in Times Square. The hotel offers 230 signature guestrooms, stacked on top of a vibrant living room plaza, a double-height space which combines the pulse of NY with a home away from home feeling. It features striking artwork in the living room by Julian Opie. With daylight from the front and the courtyard in the back it is a welcoming, active and bright space. All the functions are there: eating, meeting, working and playing, including canteenM and the Mendo bookstore. The living room plaza is divided in smaller seating areas, with furniture by Vitra. A small roof top bar with a terrace equipped with plants, lanterns and sofas, functions as pocket park on the roof and urban oasis to escape the hustle of the city.

"How beautiful it is to do nothing, and then to rest afterward." – Spanish proverb

MONKEY BAR

Architect | Dyer-Smith Frey
Location | Stuessihofstatt 3, 8001 Zurich, Switzerland
Size | 81 sqm
Completion | 2010
Type | bar

Despite the non-smoking law, the Blue Monkey restaurant in Zurich-Niederdorf features a new smoking room which is something more than a musty backroom. The concept created by the young Swiss designer duo, James Dyer-Smith and Gian Frey, is a separate smoking room, equipped with a small bar, a cozy lounge and comfortable seating. Imagine the Monkey Bar if it had been a cigar lounge in the 1920s, with classic, dark shades and bright, highly set spotlights creating a welcome, warm elegance.

"Night is certainly more novel and less profane than day." – Henry David Thoreau, American author

INDEX

PICTURE CREDITS

All other pictures were made available by
the architects and designers.

Cover front: FG+SG – Fotografia de
arquitectura
Cover back: Shamath Patil J.

246

IMPRINT

The Deutsche Nationalbibliothek lists this publication in the Deutsche Nationalbibliografie; detailed bibliographic data are available in the Internet at http://dnb.dnb.de

ISBN 978-3-03768-176-3
© 2015 by Braun Publishing AG
www.braun-publishing.ch

1st edition 2015

Editor: Sibylle Kramer
Editorial staff and layout: Helen Gührer, Maria Barrera del Amo, Jakob Grelck
Translation: Geoffrey Steinherz
Graphic concept: Michaela Prinz, Berlin
Reproduction: Bild1Druck GmbH, Berlin